90 Day Selling Success Quick Start

Brought to you by:
Brian Azar, The Sales Dr.

The Sales Catalyst, Inc.
410 Loblolly Drive
Durham, NC 27712
www.salesdoctor.com
919-620-1551

Overview

This program is for you who want…or need a structured, step-by-step system for success. You know that you can do it. You just need someone to be accountable to.

If you follow this program for the next 90 days, you will achieve the goal you want to achieve.

Program Format

You have to be committed to action for the next 90 days. We think that once you live, breathe, and achieve the goals you want to achieve in the next 90 days, you'll do this for another 90 days, then another, then another until it becomes a habit for the rest of your life.

Achieving goals is like a good drug, you want more of it so you can achieve more.

There will be a maximum of 16 people in your group. Everyone is encouraged to help each other achieve what they want to achieve. So, you'll get feedback and accountability to the group leader and everyone else in the group – 16 heads are better than 1!!

When you join the group you will be emailed a background questionnaire and a form to establish the goals you want to achieve in the next 90 days. You must share these goals with your group. That's the only way we can help!

You'll have a 30-minute conference with your facilitator prior to the start of the program to clarify goals.

You will also receive the names, telephone numbers and email addresses of everyone in your group. Please keep this list confidential.

There will be a teleconference each week to review and adjust progress and give suggestions/ideas for the next week. You are responsible for attending these programs.

Your facilitator will be available by telephone and email to help with questions in between conference calls.

Investment

Your investment in the Quick Start is $1500 in advance.

Schedule

Until First Session– Complete background questionnaire
Initial telephone call with coach

Week One – Initial teleconference
Week Six - Half -Time Review
Week Twelve– Final teleconference

Look Back This Past Year
What Are the 3 Things That You Did That Were Right

1. _____
_____
_____

Why _____
_____
_____

The results were _____
_____
_____

2. _____
_____
_____

Why _____
_____
_____

The results were _____
_____
_____

3. _____
_____
_____

Why _____
_____
_____

The results were _____
_____
_____

Look Back at This Past Year
What Are the 3 Things That You Did That Were Wrong

1. _____
_____
_____

Why _____
_____

The results were _____
_____
_____

2. _____
_____
_____

Why _____
_____

The results were _____
_____
_____

3. _____
_____
_____

Why _____
_____

The results were _____
_____
_____

The Lessons I Learned
And What I'll Do Differently

The Lessons

1. _____
   _____
   _____

2. _____
   _____
   _____

3. _____
   _____
   _____

4. _____
   _____
   _____

5. _____
   _____
   _____

What I'll Do Differently In The Next 90 Days

1. _____
   _____
   _____

2. _____
   _____
   _____

3. _____
   _____
   _____

4. _____
   _____
   _____

5. _____
   _____
   _____

Now, Let's Get Specific!

A.   For the next 90 days earnings, goal is $ _____

This should be the total of:

       Firsts   _____

       Renewals   _____

       Service Fees   _____

       Other   _____

B. My commission/sales objective is:

In order to achieve these goals, the activity plan I set for myself is:

Weekly Action Plan
To achieve these goals for myself:

		Quarter	Monthly	Weekly
1.	Pre-approach Mailings	_____	_____	_____
2.	Telephone Calls	_____	_____	_____
3.	Seen Calls	_____	_____	_____
4.	Interviews	_____	_____	_____
5.	Closing	_____	_____	_____
6.	Sales	_____	_____	_____
7.	New Prospects and Referrals	_____	_____	_____
8.	Service Calls	_____	_____	_____
9.	Centers of Influence	_____	_____	_____

My Continuing Education will include:

E.   What do you consider your major strengths, the parts of your business you do best? How can you capitalize on that strength?

F.   Which areas are causing you the greatest concern? (Please prioritize them)

___ prospecting   ___ initial interview   ___closing
___ administration   ___ persistency   ___other

Comment on Each Area:

Prospecting:

Initial Interview:

Closing:

Administration:

Persistency:

Other:

G.   Do you feel you are getting the assistance you need to meet your goals?

        ____ Yes   ____ No

Comments:

H.   Do you feel you have been recognized appropriately for your efforts?

Comments:

I.   Do you feel that management has responded to your questions and your needs?

Comments:

Expectation Worksheet

The 3 most important goals I expect to accomplish in the next 90 days are:

1.

2.

3.

The 3 most important areas in which coaching can help me accomplish goals in the next 3 months are:

1.

2.

3.

Daily Inventory (review)

List the Activities	How often?
(i.e. ask for referrals, see Centers of Influence)	(i.e. 3/day, 1/week, 60 pieces/week)

My Personal Commitment to My Future

Habit or trait that I wish to change:

Benefits to me of accomplishing this:

Three things I must do to achieve my goals:

1.

2.

3.

Date by which I will have accomplished my goal:

Three positive steps that I will take this week:

1.

2.

3.

I will accomplish this by:

Three things that would stop me from success:

1.

2.

3.

The 10 Step Sales Interview, Leading To Success

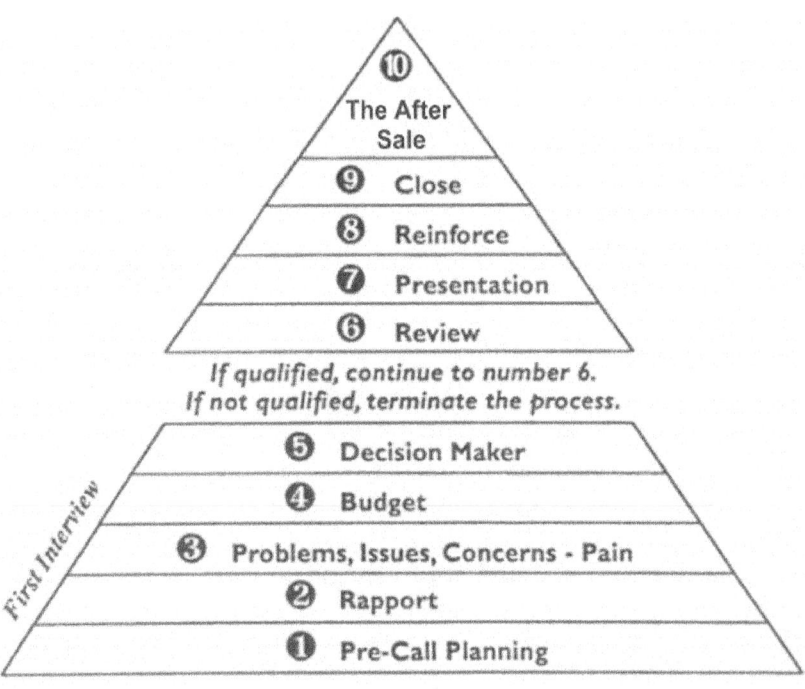

Which level(s) of The 10 Steps to Success is causing you the greatest concern? Why do you think this is so?

1. _____

2. _____

3. _____

4. _____

5. _____

6. _____

7. _____

8. _____

9. _____

10. _____

Cookbook Worksheet "A" Results from This Year
Sales I have made or plan to make this year

January	February	March
$	$	$
April	**May**	**June**
$	$	$
July	**August**	**September (TBD)**
$	$	$
October (TBD)	**November (TBD)**	**December (TBD)**
$		

TBD: Estimates for the next 90 days.

Monthly Business Plan – Actual Business

Currently   _____   _____   _____

           50%   30%   20%

Desired   _____   _____   _____

           50%   30%   20%

Past Amt of Business	Would like Future Amt Of Business	SOURCES OF BUSINESS	Direct	Intros/Referrals
		1. Telemarketing		
		2. Direct Mail		
		3. Mastermind		
		4. Networking		
		5. Natural Market		
		6. Mentoring		
		7. Spheres/Centers of Influence		
		8. Association Involvement		
		9. Retail Research		
		10. Walk-Ins		
		11. 20% Gold Clients		
		12. Advertising		
		13. Self-Promotional Newsletters		
		14. Seminars Given		
		15. Seminars Taken		

MONTHLY BUSINESS PLAN
Percentage of Business

Past % of Business	Future % of Business	*SOURCES OF BUSINESS*	Direct	Intros/Referrals
		1. Telemarketing		
		2. Direct Mail		
		3. Mastermind		
		4. Networking		
		5. Natural Market		
		6. Mentoring		
		7. Spheres/Centers of Influence		
		8. Association Involvement		
		9. Retail Research		
		10. Walk-Ins		
		11. 20% Gold Clients		
		12. Advertising		
		13. Self-Promotional Newsletters		
		14. Seminars Given		
		15. Seminars Taken		

Analysis of My Time Loss

Name:

Total # of Days Recorded _____   Total Calls _____

	Total # Hours	% of Total Hours
Meals/Breaks		
Paperwork		
Prospecting		
Selling		
Telephoning		
Travel/Waiting		
Planning		
Servicing		
Marketing Research		
Sales Meeting		

Grand Total: 100%

I plan to increase my selling time from _____% to _____%
I will gain the time by decreasing time spent on:

_____ from _____%
to _____%.

_____ from _____%
to _____%.

_____ from _____%
to _____%.

Time Management: Percentages of Time Spent

Date _____	Listening	Questioning	Speaking
Personal Calls	_____	_____	_____
Market Research	_____	_____	_____
Customers	_____	_____	_____
Suppliers/Vendors	_____	_____	_____
B. Operations	_____	_____	_____
Finance	_____	_____	_____
Employees	_____	_____	_____

Percentage of Time Spent

Date _____	Listening	Questioning	Speaking
Personal Calls	_____	_____	_____
Market Research	_____	_____	_____
Customers	_____	_____	_____
Suppliers/Vendors	_____	_____	_____
B. Operations	_____	_____	_____
Finance	_____	_____	_____
Employees	_____	_____	_____

Percentage of Time Spent

Date _____	Listening	Questioning	Speaking
Personal Calls	_____	_____	_____
Market Research	_____	_____	_____
Customers	_____	_____	_____
Suppliers/Vendors	_____	_____	_____
B. Operations	_____	_____	_____
Finance	_____	_____	_____
Employees	_____	_____	_____

Percentage of Time Spent

Date _____	Listening	Questioning	Speaking
Personal Calls	_____	_____	_____
Market Research	_____	_____	_____
Customers	_____	_____	_____
Suppliers/Vendors	_____	_____	_____
B. Operations	_____	_____	_____
Finance	_____	_____	_____
Employees	_____	_____	_____

Consciously vary the percentages during your calls and compare the results during each measurement period.

My Cookbook for Today

Dials   _____

Walk-ins   _____

Contacts   _____

Prospects and/or   _____
Existing Customers

Appointments Booked   _____

Face to Faces   _____

Referrals   _____

Futures   _____

Sold   _____

Closed Files   _____

My Reasons for Working

A_____

B_____

C_____

D_____

Knowing Your Top Clients

Platinum Clients (4%)
(To Be Contacted Monthly)

Name	Company	Product/Service	Why Platinum?	Phone
1.				
2.				
3.				
4.				
5.				
6.				
7.				
8.				
9.				
10.				

Gold Clients (20%)
(To Be Contacted Quarterly)

Name	Company	Product/Service	Why Gold?	Phone
1.				
2.				
3.				
4.				
5.				
6.				
7.				
8.				
9.				
10.				
11.				
12.				
13.				
14.				
15.				
16.				
17.				
18.				
19.				
20.				

Silver Clients (60%)
(To Be Contacted Every 6 Months)

Name	Company	Product/Service	Why Silver?	Phone
1.				
2.				
3.				
4.				
5.				
6.				
7.				
8.				
9.				
10.				
11.				
12.				
13.				
14.				
15.				
16.				
17.				
18.				
19.				
20.				
21.				
22.				
23.				
24.				
25.				
26.				
27.				
28.				
29.				
30.				

Silver Clients (60%)
(To Be Contacted Every 6 Months)

Name	Company	Product/Service	Why Silver?	Phone
31.				
32.				
33.				
34.				
35.				
36.				
37.				
38.				
39.				
40.				
41.				
42.				
43.				
44.				
45.				
46.				
47.				
48.				
49.				
50.				
51.				
52.				
53.				
54.				
55.				
56.				
57.				
58.				
59.				
60.				

Bronze Clients (20%)
(To Be Contacted Annually – Upgraded or Eliminated)

Name	Company	Product/Service	Why Bronze?	Phone
1.				
2.				
10.				
11.				
12.				
13.				
14.				
15.				
16.				
10.				
11.				
12.				
13.				
14.				
15.				
16.				
17.				
18.				
19.				
20.				

The Sales Doctor Qualifying Examination

1. What's your biggest want, need or desire, problem, issue, or concern in….?
   (Insert your line of work)

2. How long have you had it?

3. What have you done to fix it?

4. And that's worked well for you?

5. What is this costing you in terms of time, money, reputation, etc.?

6. Do you have a budget set up to solve this problem? Would you please share that number?

7. Are you the person who makes these decisions? Who, besides you would be involved?

8. Are you committed to finding a solution to this problem now?

The Sales Catalyst, Inc. http://www.salesdoctor.com   919.620.1551   E-Mail: talkbiz@aol.com
FAX: 919-620-1661

Name_____   Date _____

WEEKLY STATUS REPORT

Weather Report (1-10)   Head _____   Health _____   Heart _____

What was accomplished since last week?
(WINS) _____
_____
_____

What did not get done? _____
_____
_____

Current Challenges? _____
_____

Current Opportunities? _____
_____

I would like specific coaching on the following:_____
_____

Commitments or Goals for the Week_____
_____

TOP 6 PRIORITIES FOR THIS WEEK: CIRCLE PROGRESS

1. _____   1 2 3 4 5   Done
2. _____   1 2 3 4 5   Done
3. _____   1 2 3 4 5   Done
4. _____   1 2 3 4 5   Done
5. _____   1 2 3 4 5   Done
6. _____   1 2 3 4 5   Done

REWARDS FOR THE WEEK: DATE

1. _____   _____

2. _____   _____

3. _____   _____

www.ingramcontent.com/pod-product-compliance
Lightning Source LLC
Chambersburg PA
CBHW061237180526
45170CB00003B/1333